THE
COLOR
OF
PEACE

The Color of Peace

Nguyễn Phan Quế Mai

Black Ocean
Boston · Chicago

Copyright © 2025 by Nguyễn Phan Quế Mai
All rights reserved.

To reprint, reproduce, or transmit electronically, or by recording all or part of this manuscript, beyond brief reviews or educational purposes, please send a written request to the publisher at:

Black Ocean
P.O. Box 52030
Boston, MA 02205
blackocean.org

Cover and book design by by Janaka Stucky | janakastucky.com

ISBN: 978-1-965154-11-3
LCCN: 2025932629

Also by Nguyễn Phan Quế Mai:
Dust Child
The Mountains Sing
The Secret of Hoa Sen

FIRST EDITION
1 2 3 4 5 6 7 8 9 10
Printed in Canada

Kính tặng cha tôi: thầy giáo Nguyễn Thanh Cầm

For my father, Nguyễn Thanh Cầm.
For my family and for my homeland Việt Nam,
without whom I would not know how to sing.

CONTENTS

Introduction: Poetry, Myth and a Utopian Vision	i
The Voice	1
Tears of Quảng Trị	3
Conversation with the Dead	5
The Jungle Men	6
Babylift	8
The Lotus	9
The Mekong	11
The Fish	13
Boat Land	14
Thorns of Roses	16
Orange is Beautiful	18
Star Fruit Flowers	19
For a Veteran of My Country's War	20
Quảng Trị	22
Separated Worlds	23
With a Việt Nam Veteran	24
My Father's Bàng Tree	26
My Mother's Rice	28
Speaking with My Children	29
Grandpa	31
My Mother's Home Village	33
Uncle Thành	34
My Cousin's Lies	36
The Brick Boy	38
On Hà Nội Street	40
Việt Nam Veterans Memorial	42
A Conversation during Tết	44

The White Time	45
Talking with a Man Who Spent Ten Years in Re-Education Camps	47
Mist on the Golden Gate Bridge	48
My Mother	49
Moving	51
The String of a Đàn Bầu	53
The Garden of Time	54
The Lyrics of Stars	55
Under the Bodhi Tree	56
The Walk	58
Scent of Rice Fields	59
Frangipani Petals	60
A Dream	61
The Color of Peace	62
With Henry	64
Abuela Moreno	66
In Waiting	68
The Bombs and the Piano	70
Conversations about Herbs and Trees	72
Qinghai's Dragon	74
Manopeng Dance	75
Dialogue with Vincent Van Gogh	76
At Casa Luna	78
Night's Wings in Manila	79
At the 9/11 Memorial	81
Revelation	82
Wings	83
Epilogue: My Father Still Believed	85
Notes	93

"*Hòa Bình* were the words carried on the wings of doves painted on the classroom walls at my school. *Hòa Bình* bore the blue color in my dream—the color of my parents returning home. *Hòa Bình* meant something simple, intangible, yet most valuable to us: *'Peace.'*"

—*The Mountains Sing*

INTRODUCTION: POETRY, MYTH AND A UTOPIAN VISION

I will never forget that day in February of 2012. Silky layers of fog embraced me as I joined a group of Vietnamese and international poets walking near mist-draped mountains whose peaks seemed to soar like dragons above us. The droplets of mist tasted like Tết—the Vietnamese New Year—on my tongue. Looking out at the bay to my left, I could see hundreds of islands formed by the limestone karsts that seemed to spring from the blue water. I felt buoyant that we would be celebrating Ngày thơ, the Poetry Day of Việt Nam at such a historic location: Vịnh Hạ Long, the Bay of the Descending Dragons, a UNESCO World Heritage site. We were on our way to open the First Asia-Pacific Poetry Festival at the foot of Núi Bài Thơ, Poem Mountain, a site that reveals how poetry and myth coexist as part of Việt Nam's everyday landscape.

When I was a child, learning about Hạ Long Bay while sitting at a simple desk in a small village more than one hundred kilometers away, Poem Mountain seemed so grand. Yet no majestic image in my mind compared to the feelings that flooded me when I stood next to the 200-meter-high limestone mountain rising out of the bay like a castle with three imposing towers. In 1468, the Vietnamese Emperor Lê Thánh Tông visited Hạ Long Bay during his inspection tour to the Eastern region. Touched by the area's stunning beauty, he composed a poem and had its fifty-six ancient Vietnamese words carved into a flat rock on the mountain's southern side. Two and a half meters above the water, the words flowed without any line breaks. Over the last five hundred and fifty-seven years, wind and rain and sunshine have almost completely faded away twenty-one words of the poem. Yet Emperor Lê Thánh

i

Tông's spirit and love for literature remain in the hearts and souls of many Vietnamese who believe that poetry is an intrinsic element of natural beauty, and thus, an important part of our lives.

Although Emperor Lê Thánh Tông's poem has almost become a legend unto itself, it intertwines with the myth of Hạ Long Bay that says Vietnamese people are the children of dragons and the grandchildren of fairies. During our earliest times, when our country was invaded by foreign armies, Heaven sent Mother Dragon, together with her baby dragons, down to earth to help Việt Nam. As the dragons were descending, the invaders' ships arrived in great numbers. The dragons spewed out jade and jewels to form a chain of rocky mountains that would act as a defensive wall. The invaders' ships, traveling at high speed, collided with these walls and shattered into pieces. The invasion was thwarted and Hạ Long Bay was left scattered with unusual, beautiful rock formations. Poem Mountain, where we stood that day, is one piece of the jade from the mouth of a brave dragon.

As I admired Poem Mountain, it seemed to shift shape. Sometimes it appeared to be a tiger crouched in waiting or playing with its catch. Other times, it looked like a dragon about to take flight. If you are lucky enough to climb to the top of Poem Mountain, it will lift you up and bless you with the magnificent landscape of Hạ Long Bay. You can go there right now in your imagination. Close your eyes and open your mind to immense emerald waters, to rocks bobbing throughout the bay, to the surrounding flowers and trees, to the hundreds of karsts that rise majestically above the water. And then, a breeze will carry Lê Thánh Tông's poem to your ears:

Hundreds of tidal currents rise into vast waves
Countless mountains blend their green into the blue sky

The sound of night-drums beat strong in my heart
Calling me to build our nation with toil and tenacity
The North protected by our mighty army
Signals warning about enemies vanquished and quiet in the Eastern Sea
Throughout history, Southern rivers and mountains stand
With martial arts and letters, we lay the foundations of our land.

It is astonishing that more than five hundred and fifty years ago, Emperor Lê Thánh Tông considered literature to be a country's foundation. He was known to be a man of great vision, and today is one of Việt Nam's most admired and beloved figures. He reformed Việt Nam's military, administrative, economic, educational, and legal systems. He expanded our country and defeated foreign armies. He was a warrior but a peace-loving poet at heart.

Every year, tens of thousands of visitors come from all corners of the world to visit Hạ Long Bay, including many poets who cannot resist the urge to compose poems at the foot of Poem Mountain. As they stand there, they may not understand the ancient Vietnamese words written by Lê Thánh Tông, but they do understand—as Lê Thánh Tông did—that the Vietnamese people prefer peace to war and would rather compose poetry than fight bloody battles.

But Emperor Lê Thánh Tông isn't the only Vietnamese leader who considered poetry as the foundation of a country. Việt Nam's very first Declaration of Independence is actually the poem Nam Quốc Sơn Hà, written by General Lý Thường Kiệt approximately between 1076 and 1077 when our homeland was facing the threat of the Chinese invaders from the north. In 2009, I was commissioned by the Việt Nam Writers Association to translate this poem into English, together with the American poet Jennifer Fossenbell. Our translation below has been written onto a large ceramic vase and was displayed at the Temple of Literature in Hà Nội as part of the Poetry Day of Việt Nam:

The Southern Nation's Mountains and Rivers

The Southern Emperor rules the Southern mountains and rivers
Heaven's book has clearly marked our borders
Those enemies who dare invade our land
Such miserable loss they will surely withstand.

Today in Việt Nam, as in the time of General Lý Thường Kiệt and Emperor Lê Thánh Tông, poetry is very much alive. The National Poetry Day of Việt Nam (the 15th day of the first lunar month, or two weeks after the Vietnamese New Year) is celebrated throughout our country and attended by tens of thousands of people, young and old, year after year. People brave rain and storms to come and listen to poetry. Many people take a day off work to enjoy the art form. During poetry readings, I have witnessed the power of literature. I have seen veterans of the Việt Nam War—Vietnamese and Americans—who were former enemies, embrace and find consolation in each other's words. I have witnessed poetry as a very real utopia that reveals a path to reconciliation, unites people, and fosters understanding, empathy, and compassion.

As a poet, I am fortunate to carry the poetic traditions of Việt Nam in my veins. Poetry helps me to speak with ancestors whom I never met. Poetry opens my heart and mind to the rich world of Vietnamese myths and legends. I know that I have just scratched the surface of Vietnamese culture with my pen, and I know that I must dig much deeper to find the true voices of my ancestors.

I know too that I am not writing poetry in vain. In the current world of turbulent changes, literature can keep us grounded and our passions burning. While wars and violence still destroy the lives of countless people around the world, literature can be an ambassador for peace. As Emperor Lê Thánh Tông's poem shows us, we can begin to strengthen the foundation of our world through literature.

If you haven't had the chance to do so, I invite you to visit the magical Poem Mountain. I believe that standing there, you will discover the deep love of Vietnamese people for peace and justice. And I hope by reading this poetry collection, you will travel there in your mind, feel how poetry runs through our blood, how myths are entwined with our daily lives, and how, just like a utopian vision, all boundaries are blurred so that you and I are children of the same Mother Earth, embraced by the magnificent power and beauty of this life.

Perhaps because I was born in 1973, during the Việt Nam War, I saw with my own eyes how precious peace is. I remember so vividly that when I was a small child, I stood on the dirt road of my village in Northern Việt Nam, looking at the devastation around me and at the people who had lost family members, or their arms and legs. I told myself "The human race would not be so stupid as to wage another war. Just look at this!" As I grew up though, I came to realize that I was naïve and that humans always find excuses for violence.

Yet I want to maintain my innocent belief in human goodness. My pen is fueled by a yearning for peace and human compassion. In my debut novel *The Mountains Sing*, a twelve-year-old girl, Hương, who resents Americans for dropping bombs on her city and killing many people, later realizes that "by reading their books, I saw the other side of them—their humanity. Somehow I was sure that if people were willing to read each other, and see the light of other cultures, there would be no war on earth."

I began my writing career with poetry in 2006 in Hà Nội. I was 33 years old then and composed Vietnamese poetry in my head as I rode my Vespa from my home to my office. My love for poetry inspired me to translate many poems by other authors. And now, I am honored to present you with *The Color of Peace*, my first-ever poetry collection written in English, composed during the last many years.

In a way, the poems in this collection have helped me capture the many significant moments of my life: those that transformed me and made me feel alive, seen, or understood. I have arranged this book according to the way I have come to understand the world around me. As a result, the first set of poems confronts the direct impact of war, followed by the ones that explore inheritance and legacy, family relationships, generational impact, trauma, and resilience. The poems in the second half of the book examine displacement and identity, as well as my relationships with the wider world. As a global nomad, I have lived in Australia, Bangladesh, the Philippines, Belgium, Indonesia, and now Kyrgyzstan. As an author, I have spoken at festivals around the world. The chances to travel have opened my eyes and let me see how precious peace is. The poem "The Color of Peace" was penned in Colombia where I saw the yearning for peace from the people who had lost their homes in the civil war. Like them, I long for the day where there is no more war on this earth. And I hope you will enjoy the poems in this book that celebrate love, peace, and family connections.

Poetry is the pillar of the Vietnamese life. The beloved Vietnamese poet Phùng Quán once wrote "có những phút ngã lòng, tôi vịn câu thơ và đứng dậy," which means "during moments of difficulty, I hold on to the verses of poetry to pull myself up." Putting this poetry collection together, I can't help but recall how my mother used to sing me lullabies composed from ca dao—Vietnamese folk poetry—when I was a child. It was after the war and we were living under the American trade embargo, with little to eat. Yet my mother nursed me these ancient poems and my father told me stories to make sure their daughter would grow up rich in her soul.

Just as in Lê Thánh Tông's poem, where poetry creates the foundation of Việt Nam, my life has been built on the rhythm of language. And like a heart, poetry beats on in me.

Thank you for reading.

Nguyễn Phan Quế Mai
February 2025

THE VOICE

I don't know where the voice comes from.
Maybe from the abandoned graves
next to the house where I grew up
where rocks
were thrown onto our roof
by our neighbors
who considered us invaders
because we'd moved from Northern Việt Nam
to the South
four years after unification
but the division of more than twenty years
and the fighting, bombings, and killings
could not be buried by victory songs.

I don't know where this voice comes from.
Perhaps it's from the mango tree
in the garden where I grew up.
The tree that sang lullabies for the graves
relatives could no longer visit
because they'd escaped our country on small fishing boats
knowing they could lose their lives at sea,
or be raped and robbed by pirates.

Perhaps it's from the many women all over Việt Nam
who still wait for their men
who went to war, more than fifty years before
and never came back.

Perhaps it's from the many children
ripped from their parents shortly after their birth
by the war
who still look for home.

The voice is not only sorrowful.
It's filled with hope
for the one Việt Nam,
for peace to be settled on this earth.

The voice calls out to me
during the blackest nights.
"Get up and write," it commands.
"Our stories can't sleep
unless you tell them."

TEARS OF QUẢNG TRỊ

After the last American soldiers
had left Việt Nam
and grass had softened
bomb craters into scars,
I took some overseas friends to Quảng Trị,
once a fierce battlefield.

I was too young for the war
to crawl under my skin
so when I sat with my friends
at a roadside café, sipping tea,
enjoying the green landscape,
I didn't know how to react
when a stark naked
woman rushed towards us, howling.

Her ribs protruded like the bones
of a skinned fish,
her breasts swaying like long mướp fruit,
and her pubic hair a black jungle.

I was too young to know
what to say when the woman
shouted for my overseas friends
to return her husband and children.

Stunned, we watched her fight off villagers
who snatched her arms and dragged her away.
"She's been crazy," the tea seller said.
"Her house was bombed.
Her husband and children . . .
she's been looking for them ever since."*

How young I had been
to let myself believe that green grass
could heal bomb craters
into scars.

---

* *Notes appear at the end of the book*

CONVERSATION WITH THE DEAD

If I knew it was the last time we would speak,
I would have reached out
to hold your frail hands,
to feel my grandparents'
hearts beat inside your veins.

If I knew it was the last time I would see you
before death slammed the door of its coffin between us,
I wouldn't need you to speak
to understand the language
of our ancestors
burrowed inside your thin chest.

If I knew, I would have inhaled as you exhaled,
so I could draw into my blood
the scent of the jungles
where you'd spent your youth
fighting the war.

If I could taste
the injustice you had suffered,
I would know how to sing
to ease the grip of memories
so they would hurt you less.

Uncle Hải, I am sorry.

THE JUNGLE MEN

*For Hồ Văn Thanh and Hồ Văn Lang, who spent 41
years in the jungle of Quảng Ngãi, after fleeing the
Việt Nam War*

Media around the world suddenly crackles
with news about two jungle men—
father and son—discovered
deep inside Tây Trà forest.

On the TV screen, people pull the two
trembling, naked men out of their hut
built in the canopy of ancient trees;
they comb through the men's
forty-one-year refuge
for clues of their so-called "incredible survival."

I see the men being led to their former home
from which they ran to escape,
having witnessed how the war
had turned their family
into dust.

As cameras zoom
onto the men's faces
I see the widening whites

of their eyes howl
like flags of surrender
and the images of bombs flicker
as they fall backward in time
and make even the dead
bleed.

The men look straight into the camera
and their eyes tell me
that a war never ends
once bombs have fallen
and bullets had been sent
piercing someone's heart.

BABYLIFT *

Lifted high, flung into another world,
another country, another embrace,
this was the fate of the bewildered children,
their skin still smoldering from the fire of their evacuation.

They come home, their hair not blond, their skin not white,
their tongues bereft of Vietnamese,
but no diet of milk and butter can answer the thirty-five-year-old
      question
Who am I?

No adopted arms can replace the parents' embrace.
No DNA test can link them to their origin,
and black hair cannot think in Vietnamese.
Babylift. Over twelve thousand days of tears.
Over thirty-five years of pain,
and still, the questions have their eyes wide open.

Sài Gòn, 18 April 2010

THE LOTUS

April arrives with lotus flowers
balanced on the thin shoulders of street sellers.
I buy a bunch and bring the lotus home
where in a vase the petals radiate a scent
of an unknown land where I'm on a boat
with my grandma and my mother
who cup dried tea leaves in their palms,
their voices calming the setting sun
as my young hands row us
out onto a lotus pond
filled with white and pink flowers.

My grandma had died before I was born
but on this sampan
she shows me how to entrust the tea
to the petals so that when they close at night
they will ensconce the tea with their sleep's perfume.

I try to picture her face
but the mist around us is thick as clouds,
and as we row from one lotus to the next,
I watch how my mother's face becomes my grandma's
and how their faces turn into my own,
and how each wrinkle on our skin
is a story of our lives carved onto us by the sun and the moon.

Night comes. We sit on the sampan
listening to the flowers close, darkness melting us into one.
I don't know if I sleep on the sampan
but it is sunrise
and I am rowing my grandma and my mother,
their tender hands greet the lotus
that give us back the tea,
fragrant with their stories of survival.

When the tea has filled my palms
my grandma and my mother gather dew
from the lotus leaves into a tea pot.
"Lotus tea should be steeped with dew,
not with tap water as you always do,"
my grandma tells me, and I laugh.

And as my laughter rises, the sampan disappears
with my grandma, my mother, and the lotus pond,
and I am in bed with the sunrise
glistening on the vase of lotus flowers
whose drooping petals fall, one by one.

THE MEKONG

Legends say that nine dragons
unite their powers
to become the water
of one river
—Cửu Long—the Mekong.

I grew up near Bạc Liêu River—
the whisker of one of the dragons—
and I often saw fishermen row wooden sampans
away from the shore,
their fishing nets
blossoming across the water.

Stories about the river
flowed through my life,
men and women
who had died during the war,
whose bodies were stacked up
from one river bank to the other;
stories about how chemicals
sprayed from American airplanes
have seeped into fish, eels, shrimps, water snails;
stories of women too sorrowful to live
after their husbands didn't return from the battlefield,
who chose the water as their graveyard.

But the stories flow away. All that stays
are the voices of the children
who used to come every Lunar New Year,
their sampans filled with kumquat trees,
fruit and flowers, their laughter
rising as they jumped into the vastness
of the river's arms.

I didn't know how to swim,
though I had let dragonflies
bite my bellybutton,
so I sat on the shore,
watching them swim.

I saw then how the river swelled,
not with memories of the war,
but with the promise of spring
exploding in the laughing red firecrackers.

THE FISH

One afternoon in 1979, four years
after the end of the Việt Nam War,
My mother brought home a fish
to celebrate her children's good grades
marked in red ink.
My two brothers and I danced in our front yard,
our feet naked, our tongues
excited to taste the sweetness of fish
after months of eating boiled manioc and water spinach.

"What's wrong with this fish?"
My father pointed at the fish's large head
and its crooked body
and now all of us could see
how my mother could afford this fish:
it was too ugly for anyone else to buy.
It had gigantic eyes and two tails squirming beneath its scales.

I don't know if the seed of Agent Orange*
had managed to plant itself in me
through the flesh of the strange-looking fish,
but I remember
the tenderness of my mother's cooking,
scented with chili and ginger
picked from the garden of her spring-time love.

BOAT LAND

I am twelve,
growing up in Bạc Liêu, a tiny
town dangling on the Southern tip
of the Mekong Delta,
where sometimes a classmate disappears.

"Uyên has gone out to sea
with her family, on a boat,"
someone whispers.
None of us are supposed to know,
so everyone is robbed
of a chance for a proper goodbye
before the waves tower above
those courageous enough
to abandon the land
fragrant with the spirits of our ancestors.

At night, my eldest brother
tunes our broken radio
to catch the news
broadcast by the Voice of America Radio in Vietnamese.
My mother lingers by the window
in case someone approaches our hut.
It is forbidden for us
to listen to news from America,
but we must know.

I put my head next to my brother's
to hear the radio broadcast
about boats lost at sea,
or captured by pirates
who raped the women
and threw the bodies of children overboard.

I don't know what to think
I see Uyên laughing
the last time we played hopscotch
on the dirt surface of our school yard.

Before that, she had emptied the tears
from her eyes onto my shirt
because her father's factory
had been nationalized, taken away,
so there would be no capitalists among us.

I am twelve, and I don't understand
why our country is being pulled apart,
her arms and legs
chopped off by the sea.

To be Vietnamese
is to carry holes inside of us,
holes in the shape of boats.*

THORNS OF ROSES

For Chúc Mỹ Tuệ—Teresa Mei Chuc

You take me to this garden where the roses
open to the nectar of morning sun, each slender petal

shivering in the soft wind eight thousand miles from our homeland.
The roses listen as you tell me about your trip

out to sea on a tiny boat, sardined amongst starving
people, your mother and brother skeletons among them;

how at two years old you had to flee our homeland
into the arms of waves so tall, even heaven was dark;

how your boat ran out of petrol, and those who died
from illness or starvation didn't have the grace

of a coffin, their bodies tossed into the churning mouth of the ocean;
and how your non-stop crying made your mother

want to jump head-first out of the boat. The journey has been long
for both of us, but you are here today, with me

in this rose garden, filled with the intense
California sun, longing for homeland, and dreaming.

But the scent of roses tells me how knives
flung from the past still cut into you, and make you bleed.

Tuệ My—Teresa Mei Chuc,
we both inherited the war. We inherited the thorns of roses

that still stab us. We inherited a yearning for peace
that we knead into stories.

We are the daughters of the same mother—Việt Nam—
who live on two sides of the ocean, bound together

by thorns and by the scent of this morning's roses
and by the stories that will never set us free

until we tell them.

ORANGE IS BEAUTIFUL

In a corridor of Hà Nội Pediatrics Hospital, I stumble into a weeping mother. She is holding her seven-year-old son against her chest, trembling in a dark corner, as if being chased.

As I place my palm onto the burning forehead of her son, her tears tell me he is doomed with leukemia. The doctors have asked her to take her only child home. In a hospital where three children must share a single bed, there is no place to host another feverish body.

As I journey with the mother through the final days of her son's life, I learn her husband died of cancer and the doctors said that Agent Orange burned through her entire family. It already turned her father-in-law into smoke and ash.

"What does Agent Orange mean? Shouldn't orange be beautiful, like the sunrise, or the season's first, sweet mandarin?" She is asking me. She is asking everyone.

STAR FRUIT FLOWERS

Sài Gòn. The War Remnants Museum
(or The Museum of American Atrocities, as it was called not
    long ago).
A white girl stands, weeping in front of a photo
that shows a Vietnamese woman kneeling
in front of an American soldier
who pressed the muzzle of his rifle against her temple.

The woman wore brown farming clothes,
her palms callused.
The photo does not show, but we know,
that the gun coughed out hatred
and red blood fell onto the rice plants at the woman's feet,
staining the innocent green stalks.

But here I am next to the girl, a stranger,
who traveled thousands of kilometers to visit my homeland.
I take her hand
and lead her to the window

where a tree
leans towards us,
offers stark green star fruit
amongst purple flowers in the shape of tiny bells.

FOR A VETERAN OF
MY COUNTRY'S WAR

For TF

The day you left Sài Gòn, your head bent low during three flights where no one spoke to you, the stink of battlefields heavy on your uniform, my father wrapped himself around his younger sister inside a bomb shelter so she wouldn't scream as the bombs tore open the sky above our village.

During the months you staggered back along the pathways of your youth where your countrymen spat at and threw stones at you and your fellow vets, my mother piled stones and soil onto the river bank to repair the damages caused by American airplanes.

The year your son was born, on the other side of the ocean, my eldest brother turned one year old, learning to plant his first steps down a village road punctured by the footsteps of buffaloes, bombs, and artillery shells.

The day you sat alone, watching TV as an airplane crashed, engulfing those babylift children in fire, my father listened to the same news clutching my two brothers and me.

The days you pampered your children, thinking whether the child you might have fathered and left behind in Việt Nam was suffering abuse and hunger, my father struck me with a rod. He wanted to teach me not to waste food because he'd lived through the Great Hunger where two million Vietnamese died.

The days and nights you tried to erase Việt Nam from your memories, I held my homeland inside my chest knowing the wounds are too deep to heal.

I was 43 years old when God enabled us to talk for the first time, and your tears flowed in my eyes as we cried the rivers of Vietnamese and American sorrow that make up the truth of our war.

QUẢNG TRỊ *

The mother runs towards us,
names of her children fill her eye sockets.
She's screaming "Where are my children?"

The mother runs towards us,
her husband's name carves a hole in her chest.
She is screaming "Return my husband to me."

Time fades her shoulders.

Her ragged hair withers.
Sky spreads sunlight, dragging me along the roads
carpeted with bomb craters like the eyes of the dead,
wide open, staring.
The dry, cracked fields struggle to find their breath.

Flamboyant flowers shed their blood along the road.
Still so deep the wounds, Quảng Trị.

SEPARATED WORLDS *

Graves of unknown soldiers whiten the sky.
Children looking for their fathers' graves whiten the earth;
rain tatters down onto both of them.

Children who haven't known their father's faces,
fathers who live the fate of wandering souls,
their shouts to each other buried deep in their chests,
yet through more than thirty years, the shouts stay alive.

Tonight I hear their footsteps
coming from two separate worlds;
the hurried, trembling footsteps
finding each other in the dark;
the footsteps sucked dry of blood,
lost through millions of miles,
lost through thousands of centuries.

With each footstep I place in my country,
how many bodies of wandering souls will I step on?
How many oceans of tears
of those who haven't yet found the graves of their fathers?

WITH A VIỆT NAM VETERAN

For BW

We sit opposite each other,
a dewy curtain of hatred
replaced by the smoke screen from two steaming bowls of phở.
He sweats like a Vietnamese in the tropical heat,
like a Vietnamese, he raises his chopsticks.

The war has never stopped.
He has never forgotten the war,
and each night he must survive his own dreams.

He stays quiet,
traffic noise making waves from all four sides,
rocking us between present and past.

He can't explain the reasons for the war,
the reasons why my relatives had to fall,
and why so many children are imprisoned
in the pain of Agent Orange.

If he told me, I would not be able to touch the funeral whiteness
that has bleached his hair, and carved into his features,
sinking me deep into a bottomless, twirling tunnel.

On the nearby TV screen, another war is alive;
only an arm-span away from us, death is opening its mouth,
snatching and gobbling down lives;

only an arm-span away from us.

Only an arm span away.

MY FATHER'S BÀNG TREE

When he built our house
my father spared a patch of earth
on which he planted a sapling.

The bàng tree occupied my father's entire garden
and lifted me into my playful childhood.
As it grew into the dome of sky—vast and cool,
flocks of city birds came to sing
for only my father and me.

I grew up.
Dust and smoke filled our city;
the buildings jostled and pushed against each other;
greed jostled and shoved against itself.

Birds with broken wings
left the tree's limbs empty.
My father is small amongst the rising concrete towers.
The bàng tree is lonely amongst the rising concrete towers.

The bàng tree is my father's entire garden;
his hands, dotted by freckles, sweep its fallen leaves.
He waters it with his songs.
The tree turned into his life.

I travel far from home—
between the layers of clouds
I look down to see a dot of green fire.
My father's bàng tree is burning itself through the city,
reaching high, reaching high.

MY MOTHER'S RICE

Through the eyes of my childhood I watch my mother,
who labored in a kitchen built from straw and mud.
She lifted a pair of chopsticks and twirled sunlight into a pot of
    boiling rice,
the perfume of a new harvest
soaked her worn shirt as she bent and fed rice straws to the
    hungry flames.
I wanted to come and help, but the child in me
pulled myself into a dark corner
where I could watch my mother's face
teach beauty how to glow in hardship,
and how to sing the rice to cook with her sunbaked hands.

That day in our kitchen,
I saw how perfection was arranged
by soot-blackened pans and pots,
and by the bent back of my mother, so thin
she would disappear if I wept, or cried out.

SPEAKING WITH MY CHILDREN

For Mai and Johann

I mirror myself into your eyes, and see the blue sky of salvation.
I kneel down and believe that innocence and kindness still exist.

Your hair parts,
showing the way back to my childhood,
rows and rows of corn and sweet potatoes young as your hair,
vast rice fields fragrant as your hair.
I am five years old again, in a hide-and-go-seek game;
I find myself behind closed doors,
your tiny hands
opening the gates to paradise.

* * * *

Immense, immense the sound of your laughter and speech,
tweeting your pouting voices.
You are the adults, and I am the child.
The earth reveals itself as round one moment and square the next.
We run wildly in the field, generous with wind
and with grasshoppers, locusts, yellow flowers and red flowers.

We rock each other to sleep beside the moon and stars.
Yellow flowers, red flowers, grasshoppers and locusts.

* * * * *

The alarm clock rings in a new day with a twisted face.
In storms of movement, people stumble into each other.
Dusty road, smoky vehicle,

you call me back to the blue sky of salvation.
Washing away the dust and smoke, I am five again,
chasing fireflies under that starry night.

GRANDPA

From a hut
built with straw and mud,
Grandpa—his hands
dotted with đồi mồi,
his hair puffs of clouds—
raised his voice and called out
to a passing street seller
who had tethered
two bamboo baskets
onto a pole across her shoulders.

The seller with a smile bright
as the Mid-Autumn moon stepped into the hut,
uncovered her basket
and lifted a clay jug.
A five-year-old child
squatted on a bamboo stool, eyes wide,
watched her Grandpa
bring out a plate for the seller
to pour a liquid from the clay jug
onto it. By the rising smell

the child knew it was rice liquor.
She edged closer
as her Grandpa

struck a match,
ignited it, setting fire to the liquor.
The flame was a blue flower.

I never liked to watch my Grandpa
drink rice liquor but I would do
anything to see again
how he commanded
the blue flower of flame
to dance.

MY MOTHER'S HOME VILLAGE

I return to my mother's home village in the late afternoon
when the garden is filled with wind and the arms of banana plants.
Footprints cover the village lane and gardens
footprints that refuse to sleep
footprints that sheltered my dreams during the months and years
    I was away.

My ancestors' lullabies rustle the ancient bamboo grove.
The well is dry, my eyes are filled.

Sim flowers, where is my mother's childhood?
The childhood that saw my mother being orphaned
walking barefoot through mountains
her footsteps hollowed the afternoons.

Perhaps the Đại Huệ Mountain is greener today
thanks to my mother's bleeding young hands
the small hands that shielded herself from storms and punishment
the hands that did not forget to sing
calling the sim flowers to purple the hills.

I return to nest myself inside my mother's young footsteps
surounded by the footsteps of my ancestors
footsteps that turn into purple sim flowers, blanketing mountains
    and hills.

UNCLE THÀNH

Peeling back the layers of time, my mother and I arrive
in front of my uncle whose eighty years of life
are piled onto his bent back,
though his eyes are lively in the dark.

My mother and I have traveled our country's thin spine
crossing the mountains and rivers from South to North
to return to her birth village
to visit my uncle
but as she calls out "Brother", reaching for his hand
he shrinks back,
fear the only thing that speaks on his face.

As the oil lamp blinks away darkness
my aunt tells us about my uncle's dementia, about him venturing
for a short walk, unable to find his way back home
about him not remembering his own wife or children.

But later, as we sit under our family altar where incense smoke twists
upward, bringing our prayers to dead ancestors
my uncle talks about the land reform, recounting
every detail as if it was etched onto the blank page of his brain:

the rolling shouts of villagers, their boiling anger
the vicious ways they beat, kicked, spit at his father,

denouncing him as a rich landlord
how they ignored his father's pleading he was not guilty
that his only small patch of land could barely feed his children.

Sitting there, with the incense smoke hovering mid-air
my uncle tells me
how fear snaked itself into him back in those days.
When he was a young boy
the fear never left him, it grows and expands
so that it has become
a monster
with human faces.

Today is my uncle's funeral.
As I release a handful of earth onto his coffin
and burn incense
I see in the twisting smoke
my uncle's silent words
being written onto the sky.

MY COUSIN'S LIES

> *Nhất nam viết hữu, thập nữ viết vô*
> *A son is a child; ten daughters equal none*
> *(Vietnamese proverb)*

When my cousin gave birth to a son,
his fingers and toes opening like rose buds on her chest,
she cried her thanks to Buddha and God,
clutching his slippery body to her heart
but signing her name only as his adopted mother.

She had bribed a stranger
and a doctor with her life's savings
for them to pen his birth certificate
and make him "abandoned at birth"
and so adopted into her arms.

I can't imagine my cousin's pain
for nine months without the world knowing
the joy inside her stomach,
and how she would have to nurse the lie
that crowned her son's head
for the many years to come.

Even her two daughters didn't know
their existence was the root of their mother's lies,

that it was they who had robbed her of the right to give birth
to another child under the watchful eyes
of the two-child policy that mandated
women who dare to have three would lose their government jobs.

Who am I to judge?
But what about the men, like my cousin's husband
who hang their heads in shame for not having a son,
who blame or beat their wives for being useless
for not giving them a human with a penis,
to keep the family bloodline alive.

Who am I to judge?
My eyes can't help but see young Vietnamese mothers
aborting their babies
because they had the wrong gender,
and the hurt that throbs inside those women's wombs
more scorching
than the twirling flames of the sun
that burns itself above my head.

THE BRICK BOY

I can never forget the day
I stood at a brick factory and watched a boy
whose eyes were so clear
they let me see through his sorrows—
how badly his father
had beaten his mother who'd run away with him
to this factory to work.

I was interviewing his boss for a film.
I was about to glorify
my country's success in alleviating poverty,
but all I could see was the boy's thin back
twisted and bent under a towering pile of bricks.

I should have ignored him, stepped
away, kept my mouth shut,
but I stayed instead, waited
until his water break
then spoke to him.
I promised to come back soon
and bring him some first-grade books.
Ten years old and he wanted
no sweets, no toys,
he only wanted to know what words say.

From that day he has been the one
who appears most often in my dreams,
his skinny arms reaching backward
to tether the heavy load of betrayal
onto his bones.

I am the one who betrayed him
by trying to convince his boss
to let us make a film
that would show how he—
a successful entrepreneur—
helped send this boy to school.

I wish I could turn back time,
keep my mouth shut,
so the boy wouldn't have been sacked
for "causing trouble."

I should have known about the other face of truth:
that when it comes to greed and power
there is no charity.

ON HÀ NỘI STREET

He was so tall; when I looked up at him,
in his eyes I wanted to see
the Statue of Liberty
bathed in the sunlight of his homeland.
Instead, regrets rolled down his face,
trembling on his cheeks.

"Mỹ Lai," he said, "I just visited Mỹ Lai."
Then in his eyes, the photos he'd seen
at the site of the massacre came back:
a mother clutching her son in their deaths,
bodies of barefoot women strewn across muddy paths,
naked children, cold, and silent under the feet
of American soldiers who stood and smoked.

"You weren't involved." I shook my head. "It was the war."
Yet he shuddered. It had taken him forty-two years to come back;
each of his days filled with nightmares
and the fear that some Vietnamese
would run him down with knives on the street.

I wanted to say something else, but words were too small
so I pulled him into the Hà Nội life
rushing around us: women balancing baskets of bursting flowers
on their slender shoulders, men cycling autumn away on their cyclos,

girls giggling their way to school, their áo dàis
fluttering like the wings of white doves.

"This used to be the enemy capital for me,"
he whispered as we passed
a group of boys who stood in a circle,
kicking a feathered ball to each other,
their laughter spiraling upward.

He jumped back as the feathered ball flew toward us.
"Kick it, Uncle, kick it," the boys called out to him in Vietnamese,
their arms opening, inviting.

For a moment, the tall American man
stood as if frozen by fearful thoughts.
But as the feathered ball dipped,
spinning fast downward
his face broadened into a smile
wide, generous like sông Hồng—the Red River.

The soldier who had lost his youth
on the soil of my homeland reached his foot forward
sending the ball high
his whole body leaning toward the boys.

VIỆT NAM VETERANS MEMORIAL

Birds' song knocks on the White House;
Lincoln's smile resounds;
sunset soaks Washington in deep red.
The black wall,
fifty-eight thousand, two hundred and sixty-seven names I
    don't know,
who fired gunshots into my mind,
their boot tips still drenched with blood.
I want to bury them once more.
Agent Orange flares up its color,
and the burning Phan Thị Kim Phúc*
runs out from the rows of names.

Black, silent,
the silent answer to thousands of questions.

A tiny rose lights up a sharp pain,

a letter dim with tears that someone wrote
for his dead father.

"Father, today is my daughter's birthday. I wish you were here to blow with her the birthday candles. There isn't a day that goes by without me thinking about you. Why, Father? Why did you have to go to Vietnam? Why did you have to die?"

The rose petals wilt. Letters carpet below the Black Wall.
Their words flicker and bleed.

I hear from the gloomy earth
the sounds of American fathers
carrying their babies in their arms,
their eye sockets like bomb craters,
their hearts bullet holes. Agent Orange
lives in their bodies. Their blood
flows and drags their crying babies from their arms.

Every name on the black wall sinks into my skin
to become every face of the fallen Americans;
Washington this afternoon,
red sunset or tears?

Washington, D.C., June 2007

A CONVERSATION DURING TẾT

In my parents' living room at Tết
—the Vietnamese New Year—where đào and mai
flowers bring the color of luck and blessing to our home.

Sitting opposite me is an elderly man whose love of life sparkles on his gentle face as he tells me about his six months' walk through jungles during the war to get from the North to the battlefield of the South.

"It was 1969 and Agent Orange was raining down. Our commander told us to pee into our handkerchiefs, put them onto our nose and keep walking."

Some of the man's comrades have died from the effects of Agent Orange, their children deformed, disabled, unable to walk.

But today is Tết, and the man doesn't want to talk about bad memories. It is unlucky, so he tells me about jungle bird songs, about butterflies and flowers whose colors were so peaceful as if they bloomed for Buddha.

THE WHITE TIME

In winter's drizzling rain, in the cicada song
born out of summer heat,
I find him
standing patiently as an exclamation mark
amid the crowded stream of vehicles,
people getting stuck in their own hurry.

He alone is quiet, small,
time flowing through his palms.

I buy a motorbike taxi ride.
He takes me, unconcerned about the price.
It seems he only wants someone to hear his voice,
struggling to emerge above the high-rise towers, above the music
spewing from bars,
overcoming the hoots of vehicles
that people aim at each other as if at war.

I sit on the back of his motorbike,
listening to his story,
listening to the wind of Trường Sơn Mountains
blow through his hair
streaked with white,
listening to the Central Highlands' sun
sing on his bony shoulders,
and to bullets, cutting through the days before I was born.

The old soldier
brings far away rain drops to my eyes;
the rain carries with it the sweetness of victory,
the bitterness of the far away war
where he permanently carved his name,
and the saltiness of his worry: who will remember Trường Sơn,
and the sharpness of daily life rushing around me
as if knowing only how to reach forward,
to the front
where everyone looks ahead,

so forgetful,
forgetting,
the soldiers and their stories that need to be told.
Forgetting,
the small soldier in the middle of the noisy, crowded city
next to the crossroad, time whitening through his palms.

TALKING WITH A MAN WHO SPENT TEN YEARS IN RE-EDUCATION CAMPS

I did not hear the word "hatred" or "prison" or even
    anger in his voice.

Ten years of his life
and he told me about the train ride from Hà Nội to Sài Gòn where the conductor let him ride for free, and an elderly stranger who waited for him at the other end of the station to enquire about her son's return, who gave him money—50 đồng.

Ten years of his life
and he did not tell me about the starvation or the lost freedom
only the warm tears on his wife and children's faces
and how cold the altar of his parents who couldn't wait for
    his return,
who died from longing.

MIST ON THE GOLDEN GATE BRIDGE

For ChU

San Francisco. The climb onto the Golden Gate Bridge was steep, I was breathless, not because of the height but because behind the mist a skeleton of memory arched across Bến Hải River where my country was split into two: North and South.

Cycling next to me is a stranger I met this morning. I wouldn't have known his name had he not fought at Đăk Tô.

As we climbed the bridge, the mist cleared, revealing the black teeth of the mama-san my companion had met at a Vietnamese village and the laughter of girls who had snuck into helicopters to join his comrades' wild parties and the bodies of American men who'd died in his arms and the ghost of a Việt Cộng whom he'd shot and who followed him home and slept on his bed every single night.

We stood on top of the bridge. The sky was so clear I could see the centuries in front of us.

MY MOTHER

When I told my mother
I would go to America
to read my poetry, she
knocked her pair of chopsticks
against the boiling pot
and called out "America?"

Forty-one years before that
when she was carrying me
inside her stomach
from the sky, blackness
came and
exploded into American bombs.

My mother jumped into a shelter so small
she had to arch her back
so her baby wouldn't be squashed
against the crumbling earth.

And now, the baby—her daughter—the poet from Việt Nam
had been invited to come
to America—the land of her former
enemy to share her stories.

My mother cupped her palms
into a lotus in front of her chest
and told me she wished
she could replace guns, and tanks,
bombs, and bullets,
violence, and hatred,
with poetry.

MOVING

While in bloom
I uproot myself
from my relatives, my friends, my language.
Alone
I lose my leaves mid-air.

I sail across an ocean
so deep, the waves are named fear.
They lap against each other, they want to sink me.
They lap against each other, they want to erase me.

I plant myself among strangers.
The new garden pushes me out.
My roots start to bleed.
I am lonely among birds' voices.
I am barren among vast green.

I break away from laziness.
I shed leaves to renew.
I shake away habits.

I open each cell of my branches.
I drink each bird call.
I eat each breeze that visits me.
I learn to grow new buds.

I shudder to bloom.
I grow fruit from my bleeding roots.

I am a tree that uproots itself.

THE STRING OF A ĐÀN BẦU

A woman steps into the room
the flaps of her áo dài are waves rolling from her homeland shore
A man watches her, his face calm, gentle.

Let me help, he says, and when she arrives,
he reaches up for the collar of her áo dài
and fastens the buttons that run
from her neck, down her shoulder, and her waist.

Each touch is a fire that burns through the layers of silk,
leaving its mark on her skin and his fingers.

Even though they're only aware of each other's presence
they are not alone. They're at a bustling restaurant
where men and women drink and laugh.

When she looks up at him everything is quiet, the beer returns to its tap, the conversations back to closed mouths, the chairs under their table.

Everything returns to the order as things should be.

Just because he is next to her, her every cell trembles the way a baby first arrives on its mother's chest, like lovers' first kiss, like the music that a đàn bầu zither utters through its one string.

THE GARDEN OF TIME

I sow myself into your being.
In your hands I bud.
On your chest I grow new leaves.
On your lips I flower.
On your body I yield my fruit.

Alongside you I become a tall tree, lush,
gathering the sweetness of spring.

On the garden of our beings
we plant, nurture, and harvest,
and we grow our two names
into one.

THE LYRICS OF STARS

Walking with you under the stars
with the fragrance of summer on our tongues
I hear nothing but your voice
as if echoing across thousands of years.

I don't know where this walk is taking us,
but I know this voice, this voice
as if from another life and I know your eyes—
the sky of songs,
the lyrics of unborn poems
that tether me to the wind of this evening
where stars abandon the sky
and open themselves
onto my palms.

UNDER THE BODHI TREE

"Đợi chờ là hạnh phúc," a Vietnamese proverb tells me
that waiting is happiness.

I don't know if this is true, but I certainly feel
alive under the shade of a Bodhi tree
grown in the desert of the unknown.

Its seed was sown
from the night I stood next to you
listening to the lyrics of a song
I couldn't understand
but imagined was about love.

"Tình yêu là mật ngọt," another Vietnamese proverb
tells me
that love is honey.

I know this is not true
But I am not afraid
to wait for you under
the Bodhi tree
and when you arrive
both of us will sit
calm, under the tree branches.
Their leaves

will rustle into us
the brilliance of a blue sky
which will stay
one true color
even though
anything in this world
may change.

THE WALK

I didn't know that I was born
to have this walk
under the canopy of insect songs
under the stars that hang
like fruits from Heaven's dome.

I didn't know that I was born
to have your voice untie my thoughts
and have the palms of my heart
read by the dark.

I didn't know that I would live
to remember this walk
long after Heaven's fruits
have turned into stars.

SCENT OF RICE FIELDS

When I was a teenager, I used to wander
by myself among rice fields;
their green soothed my loneliness
and their faint scent calmed my longing
for something I couldn't name.

Boys in the South didn't like me then
I was too brown; an outcast from the North.
Daughter of teachers who worked as farmers,
I only knew how to make friends with soil, trees, and grass.

The day you stepped onto my field
and sank your hands into the mud
your tenderness touched my callused hand.
I felt the faint scent of blessing
from the rice plants around us.

And the boy who loves
this farmer of a girl
knows
that from mud
a lotus
blossoms.

FRANGIPANI PETALS

There is a speechless type of beauty
offered by these trees
whose flowers
are the rosy petals
float alongside me
as I swim.

With each stroke, I am free
from another layer
of thinking, worrying
with each stroke, I earn
a musical note
from the petals
whose voices are strange yet I have learned by heart
whose face I have not touched, but have memorized.

If there is a garden of paradise
I know it is here—as I stretch my arms
swimming the length of my longing
until I reach you.
On your lips I will whisper
"You are the garden of my poetry."

A DREAM

There is only darkness until he opens the door.
From the warmth of his body next to her, light grows.

As they whisper to each other, they become taller, stronger,
    more lithe.
Trees come to flower and birth fruit around them.
The perfume of love radiates from their skin.

As they say each other's names, the world stops spinning to listen,
    waves build towers into sky.
They rise together, higher, higher, until light
explodes onto everything they touch.

As they fall asleep next to each other, waves return to oceans,
time returns to the lock,
lovers' letters return to unwritten pens.

And the writer of this poem realizes it's only a dream that her
    two characters meet.
Yet she can taste on her lips the sweetness of their reunion
that returns every time the sun visits the sky
and the moon hangs its light onto the cloak of darkness.

Only the pen knows the secret
that from imagination, real worlds are built.

THE COLOR OF PEACE

For the displaced people at La Cruz, Colombia

The children surrounded themselves with chatter
that smelled like salsa rising up from their homes
that clung like bare bones to mountain slopes.

Their parents and grandparents stood
under a makeshift roof, telling me
how they had escaped bullets
that pelted like hail
from helicopters twirling above their heads;
the children came to me, first as timid as cats,
and then they laughed,
rubbing their hands against the rough
silk of my Vietnamese dress.

My ears still rung
from the stories' explosions
and my eyes still burned with tears
when the children reached up and took my hands.

They pulled me out to the sunlight,
and into a game of hopscotch from my distant childhood.
I jumped, bent, and picked up
the pearls of laughter that poured

out from their mouths,
and felt I belong here
to this land
torn by civil war
and the evils of drugs.

As we sprang up
together, our footsteps light with hope,
I knew the dead were watching over us,
and I saw how the color of peace
transformed into the color of laughter,
sung by the children of Colombia.

WITH HENRY

Navigating me through the crowded streets
of Bogotá, where the jobless
put themselves on show:
dancing, dressing-up, singing, begging
to appeal for some coins
from passers'-by pockets,
my Colombian guide, Henry, told me
he loved to fish with his son.

Here was a man whose travel business
was gunned down by civil war,
whose house and car
disappeared, drowned under debts.

And for a moment he seemed to forget
all of his troubles,
his eyes sparkled as he told me
about the mountains, rivers, and meadows of his homeland.

"Do you always catch enough fish to make it worth
such long trips?" I asked,
and a surprised look
 swept across his face.

"Most of the time, we catch nothing," he smiled.
"The fish are not important,
my son is, nature and our talks."

We passed a group of homeless people
whose clothes were no more than rags;
Henry emptied his pockets
into their hands.

And this time
I needed no explanation
to understand
that compassion is what
keeps us human.

ABUELA MORENO

Medellín, Colombia.
The kettle runs out of breath,
and is nursed back to life
by a pair of hands with skin
colored by storms.

"There's no day I don't think about them,"
Mrs. Moreno says, filling my cup
with the richness of her coffee.
Her words lead me
to the portraits of two handsome men—her sons.

"I thought I couldn't live on."
She turns and hands me the cup.
I feel her kindness
swell inside my throat;
she tells me about the bottomless
depth of loss
and what it means
to have both sons' lives
taken away by guns.

Mrs. Moreno holds my hands.
"Don't worry," she says,
"I am okay. I have God's love."
In her eyes, I find the light of truth,

and suddenly I am no longer
a stranger in a home
that smells like my grandmother's
even though
it's on the other side of the globe.

When Abuela Moreno reaches
out to hug me to her heart
I hear faith
speak in a language
that needs no translation.

IN WAITING

A white teddy bear sat on soft grass
looking up to brilliant petals
of sunflowers; the sky that day was a perfect blue,
filled with the wind's wandering footsteps.

Everything was perfect
but for the smell of blood
and the strewn body parts,
the smothering, twisted metal.

Flight MH17*;
this is Ukraine.

I wish I were there
to catch my countrymen,
Nguyễn Ngọc Minh and her two young children,
Đặng Minh Châu and Đặng Quốc Huy,
as they crashed down to the earth.
They had been heading home
to the city of my heart.

The teddy bear told me
he had been there, on the same flight
that those who are combing the fields
will never find him.

He is still there, waiting
for the fallen souls
to carry them home.

THE BOMBS AND THE PIANO

Our new home in Brussels
nests under the green canopies of Boitsfort
where our neighbors welcomed us
with a meal cooked with their colorful French, Dutch, and English.

Living here, in an attached house,
I can only hear bird songs and the whispers of leaves.
There are no human sounds leaking through the thick
brick walls that divide us.

Still I can hear the piano music
played by my neighbor's son
who lives two houses away.
The piano's voice travels through the solid walls
and plants seeds of a new-born spring.

Today, bombs sweep through the city I've grown to love.
Peaceful green canopies are torn to shreds.
Blood spreads onto the petals of cherry blossoms.

In the rising stench of explosions, I hear the voices
of children calling for their parents,
husbands calling for wives.
I hear terrorists cheering,
and police sirens.

I search for my family. My children run
towards me, trembling. I hold them tight
and want to put them back inside my stomach
and keep them there.

My husband finds us and his serenity embraces us
and takes us home. There we hear the piano voice
speaking, not in French, Dutch, nor English
but in the language of spring, eternal,
blossoming.

Brussels, 22 March 2016

CONVERSATIONS ABOUT HERBS AND TREES

In Jakarta, Indonesia, I find my homeland's garden tended to by Farid Hamka whose rau răm, lá lốt, húng quế, ngò gai, dọc mùng, and rau má transport me back to Việt Nam with their spiciness, sweetness, bitterness, and tanginess. The young man grows his herbs with the Vietnamese language he learns by himself, through the memories of his many trips to Hà Nội, Sài Gòn, Phan Thiết, through our proverbs that he sings under the shade of the ancient banyan tree planted by his ancestors who immigrated here from China, and who, like my own, had to survive the many brutalities of history.

"Look how trees help each other survive," Farid says as he shows me a large bayan root which has lowered itself from a branch high above to connect into the earth and become a pillar for another tree to grow on.

As he makes fresh herbal tea in his kitchen, wide open to welcome birds' and insects' songs, he tells me about the 1960s when his family and other Chinese Indonesians had to change their names, stop speaking Chinese, and erase their culture to avoid being arrested or killed. Still, many didn't survive the 1998 riots that left businesses burned and women raped.

"Unlike humans, trees help each other survive," Farid says as we savor the fragrant tea next to his koi pond. It's here I learn about his research and how scientists believe trees help each other. Through underground networks, they share water and nutrients. Through the air, they communicate, using pheromones and other scent signals. He shows me an article in which a forester claims if a giraffe eats the leaves of an umbrella thorn acacia in sub-Saharan Africa, the tree will send a distress signal in the form of ethylene gas so that neighboring acacias can start pumping tannins into their leaves to protect themselves. And how forest trees form networks where big trees pour sugar into the roots of small trees.

As I watch the koi swim, I see how at peace they are with each other. And there, in the water, I see a future where humans could go extinct if we don't learn how to live like trees.

QINGHAI DRAGON

Tempests push me above Việt Nam's flood,
I catch the tail of a surging storm
fly across oceans,
my hair pinned to swirling clouds, my feet sucked by fears of death.

The Qinghai dragon flicks its tongue and receives me onto
    the ground,
each mountain the dragon's scale,
its head the sun, its tail rolling rivers,
the Yellow, Yangtze, Mekong
pour life into my blood.

In my flesh, the waves of Qinghai Lake.
Tibetan monks summon my fears,
disperse them across deserts.
I sink into ancient lyrics.

My naked feet on the Qinghai Plateau,
I write my feelings on the mountaintop
and know that in my dream
I will be a sheep, grazing on this grassland.

MANOPENG DANCE

It must be the wings of time that carried me here to Banyiur Village, nested in the palms of the thousand rivers of Bajarmasin, and I am surrounded by hundreds of Indonesian children who speak a language that brushes against my tongue like silk and whose laughter leads me back to my childhood when I still knew how to laugh with my stomach hungry but my heart so full it was bursting.

Here at Banyiur Village, on a stage in front of us, women adorned with garlands of flowers are dancing, their bodies swaying to the music, shouts, and handclaps. Masks conceal their faces, but I can see through their eyes. I can see through their eyes how the dead rise and talk to us. In my Vietnamese village, we burn incense to talk to the dead, and here people wear masks and dance their way to their ancestors.

I have traveled thousands of kilometers to learn that we humans are alike not just in our red blood but in our flesh, how we carry forward the stories of our ancestors and how we honor them with every breath that comes and warms our lips, with every note of music that sings onto our skin.

Here at Banjarmasin, I find myself on the dance floor wearing an Indonesian mask and for a moment I am able to speak in a language that tastes like silk, and I know how to laugh again like a child who is hungry for food but who is full of hope that we, humans, are not alone.

DIALOGUE WITH VINCENT VAN GOGH

I went to The Metropolitan Museum of Art in New York to see
    your paintings
to find crowds of world travelers under your stars and olive trees.

It's funny how many of them traveled long distances to be there
only to quickly turn their backs to your paintings
so they could take selfies with your works for social media.

Hardly anyone understood you when you were alive.
Hardly anyone listened to your voice when you could speak,
but the stars and the trees did, in the ways you painted them.
Sometimes we need to be crazy to understand the sane
    world around us.

I stood in silence, my whole being tiny under the magnificence of
    your paintings.
As I inhaled deeply, I escaped into the waves of energy,
each stroke heavy and angry,
the bright colors, the rough textures,
the songs of darkness and light,
the rain that melts the earth into the sky.

I have always chased perfection
and now I see it nested among the imperfections you depicted in
    your paintings.

I wish you were alive, so I could ask about losing oneself in art, the beauty of silence and the need for humans to be alone with
> our thoughts.

And how a Dutch man could understand the joy, the pain and sorrow of a Vietnamese woman, born 120 years after him?

AT CASA LUNA

In Bali at Casa Luna, a woman stepped out of a wall. The perfume of her stories flowed through my tongue. The wall between us vanished. I heard the flowers on her hair whisper. Their colors grew onto my skin. They spoke my language.
My pen was listening.

NIGHT'S WINGS IN MANILA

For poetess Marjorie Evasco

Thousands of fireflies click open
this Manila night,
and bring us to Bohol, your home.

The river carries the breath of thick forests, mountains,
and thousands of streams that overflow towards us.
The stars are flowers that we harvest,
their light a boat-full of secrets.
Your hands pull the oars and open doors into legends:
Naga, dragons, snakes, and serpents.

"At this watershed of words
Silence is our breath and base for music."
I listen to your words sing.
On lonely white pages, you weave the dreams of others,
move the earth.

I have seen tears
soak the pages when you wrote about an injured Filipino
hiding himself from the Japanese soldiers—the killers.
But when they started to burn books
he rushed out and used his body to put out the fire.
His blood seeped, surrounded him, and protected
the words which you and I write today.

On the plows of hardship
of those who weave with words,
friendship and hope are our seedlings.

Thousands of wings of words
rise up
to offer light.

AT THE 9/11 MEMORIAL

Lines of water run down into a square basin that overflows into a smaller, seemingly bottomless square, each droplet representing the tears for nearly three thousand innocent people who lost their lives right here where I am standing.

Turn back the hand of time, and I am in Hà Nội, having just run back from work to pull my baby daughter into my arms, my mobile phone against my ears, telling my husband to please come home. On television, people are jumping from the 50th floor of the World Trade Center after the planes crashed into the towers.

Don't take selfies, I want to tell the tourists who stand around me at the memorial site. Please, listen to the tears.

Please say each name: Thomas Anderson Hobbs, Bella J. Bkukhan, Michael J. Simon, Lesley Anne Thomas, Marisa Dinardo Schorpp, Robert Walter Noonan, Khang Ngoc Nguyễn, Allen P. Boyle, Karen J Wagner, Judith Lawter Jones, Tu-Anh Pham . . .

They are resting on the wings of time, they are looking down at us, their eyes unblinking.

REVELATION

If lines of poetry could be chopped into bread
or grains of rice for the hungry,

if verses could bring smiles
to the desperate,
and fill the sad with hope,

if no tree would be cut
to print books that gather dust,

then I would feel happy
when you call me
a poet.

WINGS

For my father, Nguyễn Thanh Cầm

Larger than my hand,
the color of the sky
and a patch of red fire on its wings
the butterfly lands on a flower and flutters
as if wanting to fan away my tears.

Standing next to your grave today
I see you returning to us on the butterfly's wings
bringing the freedom of the endless sky,
placing it onto my mother's open palms.

Your hands carried my childhood,
led my adulthood through storms.
Your hand now resting under green grass,
lifting new flowers to bloom toward the sky.

Flowers the color of an eternal flame
that burns for us.
Father, please fly toward freedom
carried by millions of butterfly wings.

EPILOGUE: MY FATHER STILL BELIEVED

"Do you know that I have an uncle who's been missing since 1945, during the Great Hunger?" my father asked me over the phone a few years ago. When I told him I didn't know, that he had never told me such important and heart-breaking information, I realized that I still had so much to learn about my father. His personal history is as complicated as the history of Việt Nam itself, and like many Vietnamese people, he has had to bury many experiences deep beneath the layers of time to move on, to survive.

I once considered my father absent from my life. I have few memories of him during my earliest years growing up in Khương Dụ Village, Ninh Bình Province. Shortly after the end of the Việt Nam War—officially known in my homeland as "The Resistance War Against America to Save the Nation"—my father ventured from our home village in the North to Bình Dương Province in the South to work as a teacher. He came home perhaps once a year, and whenever he did, his friends and our neighbors would gather at our home, eager for stories from the faraway South. In our village, people always kept their doors open to welcome unexpected visitors, and my family did the same, with the result that there were always other people present for me to compete with for my father's attention.

My father was a charming storyteller, renowned in our village as handsome, his eyes always lighting up or darkening his angled face depending on what type of story he was telling. As our neighbors gathered to listen to him, a sense of admiration took root in me and grew tall and strong, like the gạo tree that stood at the entrance of our village. And like the gạo tree that bloomed brilliant red flowers, I spoke proudly of my father to friends, of his bravery in traveling so far away from home, of him being so knowledgeable about the world. Little did I know that my pride and admiration would soon be shattered.

In 1979, when I was six years old—four years after the war's end—my father came home and told my grandfather, my mother, my brother, and me that we needed to migrate to the South; the weather and our lives would be better there. The storms and floods that frequently destroyed our garden and rice field would no longer threaten us, the schools would have better resources, and food would be more abundant and easier to grow. Even though I was sad to leave our relatives and friends behind, I was excited to unite with my eldest brother, who was four years older than me and had moved South with my father two years earlier.

I helped pack the few sets of clothing that we owned, as well as our pans and pots, and got ready for the long journey that would take us more than 1,600 kilometers down Việt Nam, crossing the Bến Hải River that had once slashed our country into two, North and South, for more than twenty years. Together with my father, we traveled for several days and nights on trains and buses to reach Bạc Liêu, a town that dangled on the southern tip of our newly united country. Even though my new home was next to the town's cemetery, where grass and bushes grew wildly beside graves and fireflies flickered at night like the eyes of wandering ghosts, I told myself I needed to love that house—it was the best my parents could afford with their life savings. I told myself to ignore the cemetery and my fear of ghosts to be able to fully treasure the garden: the coconut trees that stood tall and strong, bearing heavy bundles of fruit, the pond whose surface was lit up by mướp flowers and rippled by twirling tails of fish, and the mango tree whose flowers looked like bursting stars.

On the first night after our arrival, when the joy of the reunion with my eldest brother was still bubbling in my chest, I sat down for dinner with my family. My grandfather and mother were asking my father about our new neighbors, whom we expected to be welcoming to us, just like those in our village, when our bodies suddenly jumped—large rocks were exploding like bombs above our heads as they struck our home's tin roof. There was no electricity, and as my father peered out our door into darkness, shouting at whoever had hurled the rocks toward us, fear enveloped me. Fear of the unknown. Fear that my father would not be able to protect us.

The fear only got worse as rocks continued to bang above our heads, night after night. When I ventured outside, whether to go to school, to work in our rice field, or for a walk with my grandfather or brothers, I would hear the bullies chant insults about Northerners.

It would take me years to understand the deep roots of the resentment that some of our new neighbors felt toward us. Their family members had battled against the North, and they saw us Northerners as invaders who were there to take their jobs, which was somewhat true because many Northerners were being sent by the new government to take over positions previously occupied by Southerners. Only later did I fully recognize that my Southern neighbors were suffering, too. Many were waiting for news from relatives who had been captured and sent to reeducation camps; some had seen their properties nationalized as part of the new government's effort to punish capitalists; some were attempting to flee the country by sea and join the hundreds of thousands of Vietnamese boat refugees.

My parents and grandfather were unable to discuss these sensitive issues with me, and I was too young to figure them out by myself, so I resented my father for uprooting us from our relatively peaceful life in the North to plant us in a turbulent new life in the South. All I wanted was to return to our home village, where I could climb trees with my friends, row out to the middle of the village pond with my raft built from banana trunks, ride on the backs of water buffaloes, and fall asleep in our hammock to the lullabies sung by the bamboo grove my grandfather had planted at the back of our garden.

I refused to believe my father, who kept reminding my two brothers and me that he had brought us to the South to advance our studies so that one day, we could attend universities. Neither of my parents had studied beyond high school, and it was their goal to have their children do better. My father reminded us that up until then, no one in our village in Khương Dụ had been able to attend university, and if we had stayed in the North, we would have suffered the same fate.

Clouded by anger, I failed to acknowledge the many things my father did for me: the books that he brought home for me to read, the bookshelf he built, and the long hours he worked so we had enough food to eat. I only paid attention to how hard he made us work to grow rice and vegetables and sell them on the streets or at markets. Once, my father made my brothers and me help him water our rice field after it hadn't rained for weeks and the field was so thirsty that the soil cracked. Under the intense sun, my brothers and I sweated profusely as we struggled to carry bucket after bucket of water from a faraway creek. Watching the water disappear into the parched, unquenched soil, I felt anger boil inside me. My father seemed oblivious to my feelings, his toes splayed out onto the dirt road as he walked, carrying full buckets of water tethered onto a bamboo pole balanced across his shoulders. Only now, looking back through the years, can I see how thin he had become. His cheeks were hollowed and his face wrinkled, but his eyes were still expressive and determined.

What I resented most about my father at that time, though, was how unnecessarily thrifty I thought he was. We had a fish pond, and when the fish were big enough, my father would make us dry them and eat them all year long instead of selling them. He reasoned that if we sold the fish, we would have to buy new fish at a higher price.

It wasn't until much later, when I had read enough and learned about Việt Nam's complicated history, that I spoke with my father about his past and discovered why he acted the way he did. It was fear of hunger. My father's mother, youngest brother, and uncle had all died in the Great Hunger of 1945 in horrific circumstances—circumstances that I would later fictionalize in my novel, *The Mountains Sing*. Having barely survived the Great Hunger, the French occupation, the Japanese invasion of our homeland, and the Việt Nam War, my father took nothing for granted. He always wanted to make sure that we would have food in our home so that none of us would ever be hungry again. Having witnessed so much death and starvation and recognizing how fragile peace could be, my father learned the importance of self-dependence, hard work, and resilience, and he wanted to instill in his children his strong work ethic. This is the work ethic that made me into the writer I am today.

My father's love for literature and the books he brought home enabled me to travel far and wide in my mind when I was a child. When I became a writer, I grew closer to him and my mother. In researching and writing about Việt Nam and our family's history, I came to understand the roots of my parents' trauma, the reasons for many of their behaviors, their sacrifices, and the many difficult decisions they had to make.

After the phone call with my father about his missing uncle, I talked to him several times about this traumatic period of his life, about the relatives he lost, and about the possible ways we could search for his uncle. I don't know if I will ever find my great uncle, who was named Khôi, or discover what really happened to him, but I learned many things about myself, my family, and my country when I got to travel with my father into his past. And just as he once worked so hard in his rice field, I will keep plowing my field of words until I find the answers to my questions about my heritage. As I wrote in the poem "My Father's Home Village":

Through hungry seasons, the village hill was steep,
people bending their backs, patiently tending their seeds,
their gazes haunted by cracked fields.
My father still believed, still ploughed and hoed,
the village roads fragrant again with the scent of freshly cut hay.
Storms came, destroyed the gạo tree at the village gate,
but the bamboo grove gave birth to new seasons of young plants.

During the past many years, my father was my best friend. He read every piece of my writing in Vietnamese and shared his life experiences with me. His eyes lit up whenever I talked about my books, my readers, and the wonderful places that host my readings. In April 2024, when I was in the United States for a book tour, he suddenly became sick and was diagnosed with a terminal illness. I canceled the tour and flew home to be with him. We had nearly three months together in Sài Gòn. It was the hardest time of my life, but also the most transformative. During his last weeks in the hospital, I would sit by his bed and work on this book whenever he slept.

My father, Nguyễn Thanh Cầm—a survivor of several wars, a believer in peace—passed away on 24 June 2024 at age eighty-six. He wrote poems but never published them. He was a poet at heart and inspired me to become a poet. This book, therefore, is dedicated to him.

After my father's passing, I could not write about him for many months. Grief was a sharp knife that stayed deep under my skin. I was afraid if I ventured near it with my pen, it would slash me open. It was only during a writing residency in Huế seven months later, in January 2025, that I was able to write the very last poem in this collection, "Wings."

And I know that my father is not gone. He bears witness to many poems in this collection: "The Voice," "The Mekong," "The Fish," "My Father's Bàng Tree," "Grandpa," "A Conversation during Tết," "Moving," and "Wings."

Thank you, Father, for the strength and the light you continue to give me. Con yêu Cha rất nhiều!

NOTES

p.4 — During the Việt Nam War, American aircraft dropped over 5 million tons of bombs on Việt Nam, 2 million tons on Laos and half a million tons on Cambodia. Many of those killed are innocent civilians. Tens of thousands of explosives are still being found each year. Today, children still die from unexploded bombs.

p.8 — "Operation Babylift" was carried out during the last days of the Việt Nam War. According to information from the American side, more than 3,300 children considered to be orphans were airlifted from the South of Việt Nam in 1975 and were adopted in the United States and several other countries such as Australia, France, and Canada. However, some of those children were not orphans and many have returned to Việt Nam to find their birth parents, with very little hope.

p.13 — During the Việt Nam War, the US military sprayed approximately 19.5 million gallons of herbicides in South Việt Nam to clear vegetation that was believed to conceal enemy troops and that provided food for them. The most widely used of those defoliants, Agent Orange, contains dioxin—one of the most toxic substances known to science. Apart from causing cancer and many other serious diseases as well as birth defects in humans, Agent Orange destroyed five million acres of Vietnamese forests and damaged some 500,000 acres of cropland. It continues to kill people today.

p.15 — Between 1975 to 1992, hundreds of thousands Vietnamese escaped Việt Nam by boats. Many lost their lives in the vast oceans. Some of my classmates disappeared at that time and even now, I don't know what happened to several of them.

p.22 — Quảng Trị was one of the bloodiest battle fields during the Việt Nam War.

p.23 — The Việt Nam War ended 50 years ago, on 30th April 1975, yet hundreds of thousands of families are still looking for the remains of their loved ones.

p.42 — Phan Thị Kim Phúc is the child subject of a Pulitzer Prize-winning photograph taken during the Việt Nam War on June 8, 1972, by photographer Nick Út. The photo showed her running naked and crying, after being severely burned by napalm. During the war, nearly 400,000 tons of napalm was droped onto Việt Nam by the US military.

p.68 — On July 17, 2014, Flight MH17 of Malaysia Airlines was shot out of the sky and crashed in eastern Ukraine, killing all 298 passengers and crew aboard. An investigation led by the Dutch Safety Board concluded that a Russian-made missile brought the plane down.

ACKNOWLEDGEMENTS

A writing residency in Huế—the imperial citadel of Việt Nam—gave me the chance to finalize this manuscript. Grateful thanks to the Diasporic Vietnamese Artist Network and the Henry Luce Foundation for their faith in my writing.

I am grateful to generations of poets whose work inspired me to become a writer. My parents read me poetry when I was young and brought home many books of poetry for me. I am very fortunate that the writers Bruce Weigl, Wayne Karlin, Paul Christiansen, and Jennifer Fossenbell read earlier versions of this manuscript and provided valuable suggestions. Thanks to my agent Julie Stevenson who has enabled my work to travel far.

I am grateful to Black Ocean for giving this book a home. It's an honor to be supported by the poets whose writing I admire and who worked with me in editing this book: Janaka Stucky and Carrie Olivia Adams. It seems like a dream that on 3 November 2024, my dear friend and peace activist Ron Carver wrote to me, asking if I would consider translating more of my Vietnamese poetry into English. When I answered I was actually writing poetry in English and had a manuscript, Ron introduced me to Black Ocean, who decided to devote an incredible amount of time on speeding up their publishing proccess so that *The Color of Peace* would be printed in time to commemorate the 50th anniversary of the end of the Việt Nam War.

Sincere thanks to the editors of the following publications where some poems in this collection were first published:

"Tears of Quảng Trị" first appeared in *Terminus Magazine*, a publication of Georgia Tech University, Issue 11, 2014, and then in the anthology *Let Me Tell You a Story*, edited by Dr. Suzanne Con-Boy Hill, 2016. It was also published by *eMerge Magazine* and nominated for a Pushcart Prize.

An earlier version of "On Hà Nội Street" first appeared in *Moving Worlds: A Journal of Transcultural Writings*, University of Leeds, Volume 15, Number 1, 2015, 'Translating Southeast Asia' issue, and then in the anthology *Let Me Tell You a Story*, edited by Dr. Suzanne Con-Boy Hill, 2016.

"For a Veteran of My Country's War" first appeared in the anthology *Alcatraz*.

"The Fish" was previously published in *The Best Asian Poetry* (2021), Kitaab, Singapore, and later published in *Convergence: Poetry on Environmental Impacts of War*.

"Qinghai Dragon" first appeared in the anthology *Poetry Across the Languages: Dialogue and Translation between Chinese and International Poets*, The Beijing Normal University, 2016.

"With Henry" first appeared on the anthology *Quixotica: Poems East of La Mancha*, selected and published by Chameleon Press (2016) and sponsored by the Spanish Consulate General in Hong Kong and Macao.

"The Color of Peace" and "Mrs. Moreno" first appeared in *Vietnam-US Magazine*, dated 12/6/2014, and then in the anthology *Let Me Tell You a Story*, edited by Dr Suzanne Con-Boy Hill, 2016.

"Moving" first published in *Women, Wit & Wisdom—Multilingual Poetry Anthology of Women Poets* (India, 2018).

"My Father's Bàng Tree" first appeared in a magazine that features 10 Vietnamese / Vietnamese diaspora writers accompanied by Vietnamese visual artists, published by the Miami Book Fair as part of the 2022 National Endowment for the Arts Big Read Program.

"Quảng Trị," "Babylift," "Separated Worlds," "Việt Nam Veterans Memorial," "With a Việt Nam Veteran," "The White Time," "My Mother's Rice," and "Speaking with My Children" first appeared in *The Secret of Hoa Sen*. Grateful thanks to BOA Editions, Peter Conners, and Bruce Weigl for granting me the permission to reprint these poems in this collection.

My introduction of this book is an adapted and expanded version of the essay "Poetry, myth and a utopian vision", which I originally wrote in Vietnamese for the *Literature Newspaper*. The essay was translated into English by myself together with the poet David McKirdy.

My epilogue of this book is an adapted and expanded version of my essay "My Father Still Believed" which was commissioned and first published by *Stranger's Guide* magazine.

Last but not least: Thank YOU for reading my books, and for changing my life with your support.

ABOUT THE AUTHOR

Nguyễn Phan Quế Mai's poetry in Vietnamese has been written into popular songs and won top literary prizes in Việt Nam including the Poetry of the Year Award 2010 from the Hà Nội Writers Association. She is the author of thirteen books in Vietnamese and English, including the internationally bestselling novels *The Mountains Sing* and *Dust Child*. She has been honored with numerous international awards including the PEN Oakland/Josephine Miles Literary Award, the BookBrowse Best Debut Award, the International Book Award, the Lannan Literary Fellowship in Fiction, as well as Runner-up for the Dayton Literary Peace Prize. Quế Mai's writing has been translated into more than twenty-five languages and has appeared in major publications including *The New York Times*. An advocate for Vietnamese literature, she is the translator of eight books and was named by Forbes Việt Nam as one of 20 inspiring women of 2021. She has a Ph.D in Creative Writing from Lancaster University in the United Kingdom. *The Color of Peace* is her first poetry collection in English. For more information: nguyenphanquemai.com